Nail Art!

With over 20 amazing nail designs to wow your friends and family!

priddy books

Contents

With 25 designs to choose from, you're spoiled with choices. Let's get painting!

Technique pages: Dotting Tool, p10; Nail Stencils and Stickers, p22; Sponge, p45.

Nail Beauty Box

There are only a few basic items you'll need to get started on the nail art in this book. You can collect more nail polish, tools, and embellishments along the way!

Nail Polish
You'll need a clear top coat and a selection of colors to create the designs in this book. It is very useful to have a white and a black nail polish, too!

Nail Clippers
To cut nails.

Nail File
To shape nails.

Nail Scissors
To cut and shape nails.

Cotton Pads
Use with nail polish remover to remove nail polish.

Cotton Swab
Use with nail polish remover to clean up polish around the nail.

Nail Polish Remover
Use with cotton pads or a cotton swab to remove nail polish.

Cuticle Sticks
To push your cuticles back and clean up the nail area.

Dotting Tools
To draw and dot polish onto your nails. See page 10 for the technique.

Tape
Use instead of nail stencils.

Makeup Sponges
Needed for color-fade designs. See page 45 for the technique.

Bobby Pin
An alternative to a dotting tool.

Nail Art Pen
For drawing designs. Can be used instead of a dotting tool.

Nail Gems
Can be stuck to wet nail polish.

Toothpicks
An alternative to a dotting tool. These can also be used for very fine details.

Nail Stickers
For quick fix nail art. See page 22 for the technique.

Nail Stencils
For precise nail designs. See page 22 for the technique.

Loose Glitter
To add sparkle. See page 29 for the All That Glitters design.

Preparing Your Nails

Before you start to paint any designs, it is important to prepare your hands and nails to make sure they are clean, trimmed, and ready to look their best!

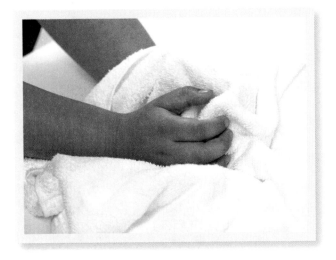

1 Wash your hands with warm soapy water and clean under your nails with a nail brush.

2 Carefully push back your cuticles using a cuticle stick.

3 Trim your nails with a pair of scissors or nail clippers. Ask an adult for help if you need it.

4 Shape your nails with a nail file so that they have rounded edges.

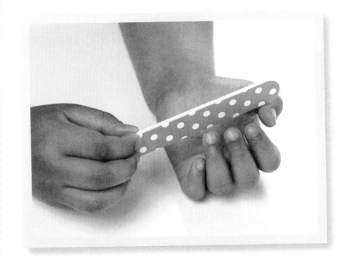

Basic Tips

Follow these basic instructions for every nail art design, and you'll have perfectly polished fingernails!

Get a friend to help you paint your other hand.

 1 Make sure not to have too much nail polish on your brush.

 2 Use long strokes to paint a coat of nail polish. Start in the middle of the nail, with one stroke from the cuticle to the tip. Paint another stroke on each side of the first to cover the whole nail.

 3 Make sure your nail polish is completely dry before moving on to each new tutorial step. Don't rush your designs—the more care you take, the better they'll be!

 4 All designs need a clear top coat. Paint one coat after the final step for every design unless stated otherwise.

Take it slow!

One Last Thing!

The tutorial steps in the book are shown upside-down as this will be your view when painting your own nails. Your finished nail art will then be the right way up for everyone to admire!

Tip

Base

Color Basics

Get started by experimenting with color . . .
Try out these creative combinations to
prepare yourself for some serious nail art!

Pick bold colors that really pop!

Rainbow Brights

**What you need: Red, orange,
yellow, green, and blue nail polish.**

Thumb --------- Middle finger --------- Pinkie

1 Follow the pattern above to paint
the nails on both your hands.

2 Apply another coat of each color.

Tip: You could use a glitter
top coat for a sparkly shine!

Why not try using more
colors to create a rainbow
effect across both hands?

Following the image, paint each
nail a different color. You'll need
10 different colors in total and you
may need to apply two coats.

Tonal Pink

This sophisticated design uses different shades of the same color—just pick your favorite and get painting!

What you need: Five nail polishes that are different shades of one color.

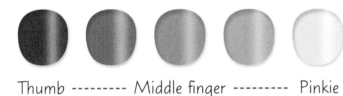

Thumb --------- Middle finger --------- Pinkie

Hint: A glossy top coat completes the look!

Amazing Tones

Get inspiration for more tonal designs from these color palettes.

Sunset Sky

Into the Deep

Green Hues

Shiny Metallic

Berry Magic

Why not pick colors that match your outfit?

Using a Dotting Tool

A dotting tool is used for adding dots and designs to your nails. They are cheap to buy and a must for all nail art fans.

1 Decide which end of the tool to use (the larger end can be used for dots whilst the smaller end is best for drawing delicate designs). Pour a little nail polish onto a piece of cardstock and dip the end of the tool into it so it is covered but not dripping.

2 Dot the tool quickly onto the nail to create a dot or use it like a pen to create shapes.

3 Re-dip into the nail polish after every two or three dots or patterns for a clear design.

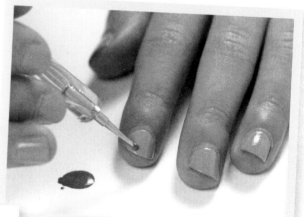

4 Use a cotton pad soaked in nail polish remover to clean your dotting tool between colors or when you have finished using it.

Don't have a dotting tool? Try one of these!

Bobby pins

The eraser on the end of a pencil

Toothpicks

The end of a paintbrush

Get Dotty!

Now that you've learned the dotting technique, try out this pretty polka dot design. Pick two colors and get practicing!

What you need:

- Pink nail polish
- Purple nail polish
- Dotting tool

Perfect party nails!

1 Paint your nails using pink nail polish.

2 Use your dotting tool to make large dots on each nail using purple nail polish.

Tip: Use a cotton swab to remove excess polish.

Try out more polka dot patterns to get really dotty!

Mix and Match

Paint a different-colored base coat on each nail to mix up the pattern!

Roll the Dice

Use black-and-white nail polish to make this super-cool dice design!

Sweet Treats

Doodle candy characters to use
as inspiration for colorful nail designs!

Doodle like crazy!

Zzz

13

Poodle Doodle
Give this dog a super poodle hairdo.

Flower Power

This cute flower design is the perfect springtime treat and is very simple to do. What color base will you choose?

What you need:

- Red nail polish
- White nail polish
- Yellow nail polish
- Dotting tool

This design looks fab with any color base or center!

Blue

Pink

Yellow

1

Paint your nails using red nail polish.

2

Using your dotting tool and white nail polish, add five overlapping dots in a circle in the center of each nail.

Tip: Press your dotting tool harder for larger dots.

3

Clean your dotting tool and use it again to add a yellow dot to the center of the petals you've created.

Doodly Googly

Turn these googly eyes into crazy creatures!

Googly Eyes

Go googly crazy with this fun design.
How many eyes can you fit on each nail?

What you need:

- Orange nail polish
- White nail polish
- Black nail polish
- Dotting tool

Smile for the camera!

1

Paint your nails using orange nail polish.

2

Use your dotting tool and white nail polish
to add two pairs of dots on each nail.

Tip: Make the dots
different sizes for a
more random effect.

3

Clean your dotting tool and use it again
to add black dots on top of the white.

What's Your Signature Style?

Ever wondered what your signature style is?
Complete the quiz below to find out
which nail art design would suit you best!

Question 1
Which print do you like the most?

a)  b) c)

Question 2
What is your favorite animal?

a) b) c)

What will your style be?

Question 3
Complete this sentence:
I can't live without my . . .

a) . . . favorite T-shirt.
b) . . . sparkly sneakers.
c) . . . skinny jeans.

Question 4
Which sunglasses do you prefer?

a) b)
c)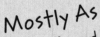

Question 5
What color is your favorite dress?

a) Black-and-white
b) Pink, of course
c) Rainbow-colored

Mostly As
Your style is simple and stylish—you never look over the top. Go for a chic design like Get Dotty on p11.

Mostly Bs
Your style is totally cute and always sparkly. Choose a pretty design like Glitter Fairy on p31.

Mostly Cs
You love adventures and trying new things—you're a trend setter! How about Shocking Squares, on p24?

Mini Mustaches

Give each nail a mini mustache with this cute and stylish design.

1

Paint your nails using turquoise nail polish.

2

Use your dotting tool and black nail polish to add two dots in the middle of each nail. Go onto step 3 without letting the polish dry.

3

Use the smaller end of your dotting tool (but with no polish this time) to pull the wet dots into little flicks to create the mustache shape.

What you need:

- Turquoise nail polish
- Black nail polish
- Dotting tool

Tip: Use a black nail art pen for a more precise design.

Pretty Confetti!

This pretty pattern is a great way to impress your friends and family at birthday parties and celebrations.

This design looks great with any color combination!

What you need:

- Light blue nail polish
- Purple nail polish
- Pink nail polish
- White nail polish
- Yellow nail polish
- Dotting tool (or use one of the alternatives)

It doesn't matter how neat you are. The more random, the better!

Let's Get Started:

1

Paint your nails using light blue nail polish.

2 Use the smaller end of your dotting tool and purple nail polish to draw one or two squiggles on each nail.

4 Next, use the larger end of your dotting tool and white nail polish to add a few dots between the shapes.

3 Clean the dotting tool and use it again to add two or three pink squiggles.

5 Clean the dotting tool and use it again to add yellow dots. Smaller dots will fill in gaps!

Graffiti Brush

Try this fab splatter pattern!

What you need: A selection of bright nail polishes, a toothbrush (with same-length bristles).

1   Paint your nails with a base color.

2   Paint your next color onto the bristles near the end of the toothbrush.

> Make sure to clean the toothbrush after each coat—use nail polish remover and paper towel.

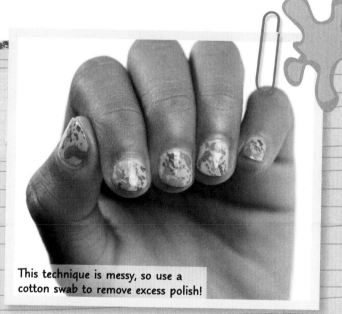

This technique is messy, so use a cotton swab to remove excess polish!

3   Holding the toothbrush at an angle, carefully dab the brush onto your nails to create splodges.

4   Once dry, apply as many other colors as you like in the same way to create a layered effect.

Using Nail Stencils

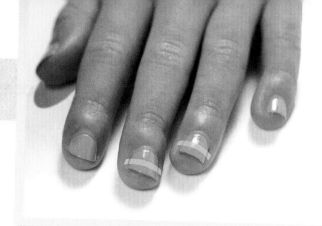

Nail stencils help create precise designs. You will find strips, zigzag strips, stars, and heart stencils on your sticker sheet.

⭐ **1** Paint your nails using any color nail polish. Leave your nails to dry.

⭐ **2** Take a stencil and position it on your nail in the place where you would like to create your design. Press it down firmly to seal all the edges.

⭐ **3** Choose a second nail polish color and paint over the whole nail, or the section where you want the design to appear.

⭐ **4** After 5 seconds, peel off the stencil carefully in an upward direction, then throw it away.

⭐ **5** Repeat with more strips if required and finish with a clear top coat.

> You can make your own strips using tape—cut small sections at about 2 mm thick before you start your design so they're ready when you need them!

Using Nail Stickers

There are hundreds of stickers on the sheets in this book. Use them to create amazing design combinations!

⭐ **1** After painting a base coat, peel off a sticker and position it on your nail.

⭐ **2** Press the sticker down firmly and hold for a few seconds.

⭐ **3** Paint a clear top coat to seal the sticker and add a glossy finish.

Mix and match the stickers to make your own awesome designs!

 Star   Heart   Musical Note Spots

50/50 zigzag

This is a design of two halves.
Pick bold colors to make it stand out.

 1

Paint your nails using
green nail polish.

 2

Apply a zigzag strip
down the middle of the nail.

What you need:

- Green nail polish
- Gray nail polish
- Zigzag strips

 3

Paint the exposed nail area
using gray nail polish.

 4

Peel off the strip carefully
in an upward direction.

Shocking Squares

This geometric design is perfect for creative nail artists. Once you've got the hang of using the strips, it's super-simple!

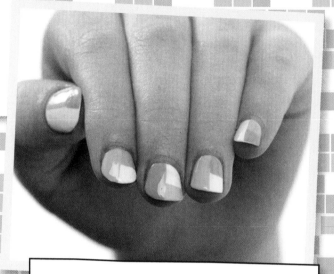

If you are using tape, cut 30 strips before you start.

What you need:

- White nail polish
- Yellow nail polish
- Green nail polish
- Stencil strips

Let's Get Started:

The tutorial shows the steps for your thumb and pinkie finger. Use the images below as a guide for your other fingers.

Thumb ---------------------------------- Middle finger ---------------------------------- Pinkie

1

Paint your nails using
white nail polish.

 2

Apply a strip vertically
from base to tip, as shown.

 3

Paint the exposed nail area
using yellow nail polish.

 4

Peel off the strip in
an upward direction.

 5

Next, apply a strip
horizontally, as shown.

 6

Apply another strip
vertically, as shown.

 7

Paint over the larger yellow area
using green nail polish.

 8

Peel off the strips one by one,
in an upward direction.

Lovely Ladybugs

Get closer to nature with this cute ladybug design! It also looks great on just one nail, with your other nails painted black.

What you need:
- Red nail polish
- Black nail polish
- White nail polish
- Dotting tool

After each step, make sure your nails are completely dry.

Let's Get Started:

1 Paint your nails using red nail polish.

2 Use black nail polish to paint the tips of your nails.

Tip: Start with your brush at one side and paint across your nail.

3

Use your dotting tool and black nail polish to draw a line down the center, as shown.

Tip: Make sure there isn't too much polish on your dotting tool.

 4

Use your dotting tool again to add three black dots in the spaces on either side of the line.

 5

Clean your dotting tool and use it again with white nail polish to add two white dots for the eyes.

 6

Clean your dotting tool and use it again with black nail polish to add two smaller black dots as eyes.

BUZZ BUZZ

Try this buzzy bee design and you'll stand out from the crowd!

What you need: Yellow nail polish, black nail polish, stencil strips.

1   Paint your nails yellow. You will need two coats.

2   Apply three strips, as shown. The bottom strip should touch your cuticle and the top strip should hang over the tip.

3   Paint over your whole nail using black nail polish.

4   Carefully peel off the strips in an upward direction. Repeat steps 2 and 3 for every nail.

Wow! What a striking design!

Sparkly Star

Get in the sparkly spirit
and finish this star pattern!

All that Glitters

What you need:
- Pink nail polish
- Clear top coat
- Loose glitter
- Scrap paper

This super-sparkly nail art will add some glam to your look!

This design will look lovely with any pastel shade...

Blue   Yellow   Purple

Paint your nails using pink nail polish. Move on to step 2 without letting the polish dry.

Place your hand on a piece of scrap paper, and sprinkle glitter over your fingernails. Shake your hand to get rid of any loose glitter.

Tip: Remember to add your top coat after this design as it will seal in the glitter.

Beautiful Bling!

Oh, so sparkly!

Finish this ring with a huge diamond!

30

Glitter Fairy

You'll be the envy of your friends with this loveable design.

What you need:

- Light pink nail polish
- Glitter nail polish
- Heart stencils

Paint your nails using light pink nail polish.

Paint over only the heart area using glitter nail polish.

Apply a stencil to the middle of each nail. Press it down gently so there are no gaps for polish to leak into.

Peel off the stencil in an upward direction.

Tip: Only peel off the part of the stencil that you want to use.

Cookie Creations

Decorate the heart cookies and get inspired for some super-sweet nail designs!

Which Nail Art Suits You?

Mix it up! Pick color and style combinations to help
you decide which nail art design to pick today!

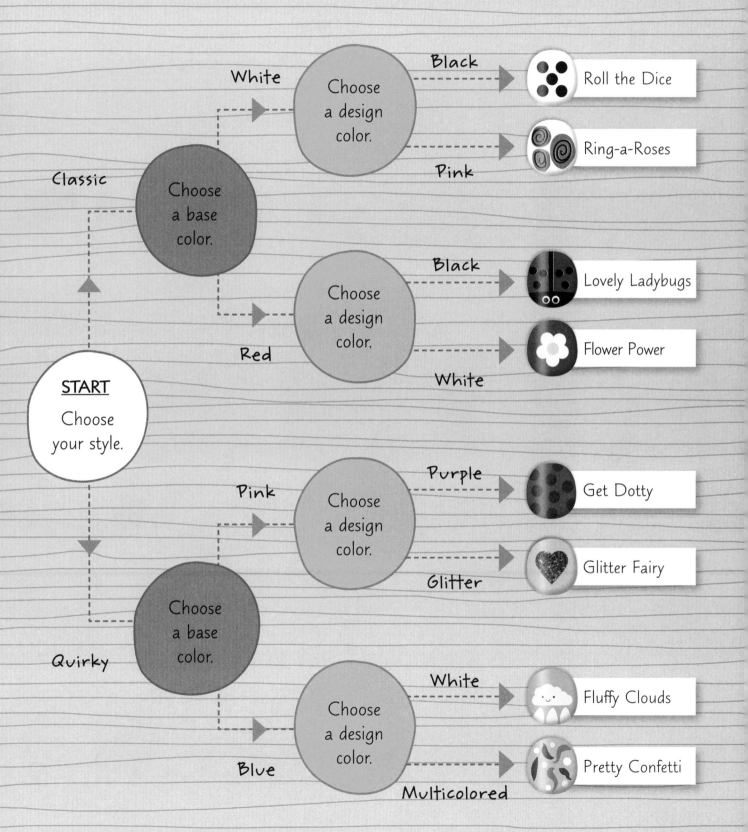

White → Choose a design color.
Black → Roll the Dice
Pink → Ring-a-Roses

Classic → Choose a base color.

Red → Choose a design color.
Black → Lovely Ladybugs
White → Flower Power

START
Choose your style.

Pink → Choose a design color.
Purple → Get Dotty
Glitter → Glitter Fairy

Quirky → Choose a base color.

Blue → Choose a design color.
White → Fluffy Clouds
Multicolored → Pretty Confetti

wild at Heart

This leopard print is perfect for creative nail artists. You can freestyle the design as you wish to get really crazy effects!

What you need:

- White nail polish
- Red nail polish
- Black nail polish
- Dotting tool

It doesn't matter how neat you are. The more random, the better!

Let's Get Started:

The leopard print looks awesome in any color combination—which will you choose?
How about a different color on each nail?

Red

Blue

Purple

Yellow

1

Paint your nails using
white nail polish.

2

Use red nail polish to create three to
six irregular blobs on each nail.

Tip: Be careful to leave enough
space for the next step.

3

Use your dotting tool and
black nail polish to create C-shapes
on either side of each red blob.

4

Use the dotting tool again
to add more black C-shapes and
small blobs into the gaps.

Sparkly Giraffe

Why not try another animal print?
This giraffe design is super-shiny!

The layer of glue will mean that
you can peel off the design easily
instead of using nail polish remover!

What you need: craft glue, paintbrush, yellow nail polish, brown glitter nail polish.

⭐ 1 Paint your nails with a
thin layer of craft glue
using a thin paintbrush.
Wait until it's dry.

⭐ 2 Paint your nails with
two coats of yellow
nail polish.

⭐ 3 Using your glitter nail polish,
add irregular blobs to cover
each nail. Make them larger
than the leopard print ones.

⭐ 4 Finish with a glossy top coat
to seal in your sparkly design.

Cloud Characters

Give each cloud a cute face. Then doodle the weather!

Keep smiling!

Fluffy Clouds

Float away with this dreamy design—the friendly cloud faces will brighten up any rainy day!

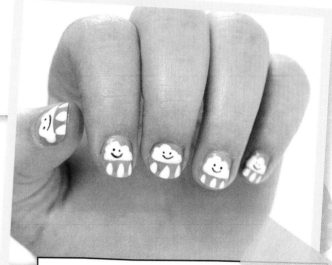

If you don't have a nail art pen, try using a toothpick.

What you need:
- White nail polish
- Blue nail polish
- Dotting tool
- Black nail art pen

Let's Get Started:

1

Paint your nails using white nail polish. This will make the next layer really pop.

4 Use your dotting tool again to add three lines below each cloud for the raindrops.

2 Paint your nails using blue nail polish.

Tip: Go right to the edges of your nails so you don't see the white underneath.

5 Use a black nail art pen or a toothpick with black nail polish to add a smiley face to each cloud.

3 Use your dotting tool and white nail polish to create clouds by making lots of dots and joining them in a group.

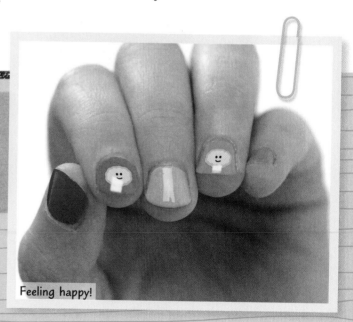

Feeling happy!

Smiley Skies

How about trying rainbow nails with your smiley cloud stickers?

What you need: Red, orange, yellow, green, and blue nail polishes, four cloud nail stickers.

1 Paint your nails using rainbow colors. Go to page 8 to remind yourself of the rainbow designs.

Go cloud crazy and add a sticker to every nail—or try just one on the ring fingernail of each hand.

2 Apply a cloud nail sticker to your pointer fingernails and your ring fingernails on both hands, as shown.

3 Finish with a clear top coat on every nail to seal in the design.

Just Rosy

Floral nail designs are super-chic.
Get in the spirit with some flower doodles!

41

Ring-a-Roses

Go girly with this flower design. Pick any combination of rosy colors— whatever takes your floral fancy!

What you need:

- White polish
- 3 different colored polishes for the roses
- Black nail art pen

Let's Get Started:

1

Paint your nails using white nail polish.

2

Use one of your colored nail polishes to add a large blob on each nail.

Tip: Use the tip of your brush to create a blob!

3

Use another color nail polish to add a second blob next to the first one, a little smaller than the first one, as shown.

 5

Using your black nail art pen, draw a swirl in the largest blob.

Tip: To draw the swirl, start in the middle and spiral outward.

 4

Use your third color nail polish to add a final blob.

6

Draw the other two swirls with your nail art pen to finish the design.

Creative Swirls

Let your creativity out and freestyle your own version of this curly, swirly design.

Tip: It doesn't matter if your swirls go over the spot stickers. The crazier, the better!

What you need: White nail polish, spot nail stickers, black nail art pen.

 1 Paint your nails using white nail polish, or any other light color.

 3 Use your nail art pen to add random swirls all over each nail.

 2 Pick two or three spot stickers and apply them to each nail.

 4 Finish with a glossy top coat to seal in the design.

Beachy Doodles

Take a break from painting to doodle cute characters on this sandy beach!

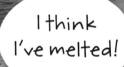

I think I've melted!

Using a Sponge

This technique can be used to create color-fade designs. A makeup sponge is perfect, or use a small piece cut from a larger sponge.

Paint a top coat or use the effect as a background for another design.

1. Paint your nails using white nail polish to make the colors on top stand out.

2. Take a sponge and paint your chosen nail polish directly onto the sponge in lines to create the color-fade effect, or in any other design you want.

3. Dab the sponge onto your nail. Don't worry if you get polish on your skin.

4. Clean away any messy polish around your nail with a cotton swab and nail polish remover.

5. Repeat on each nail until you have the effect you like.

Try out these sponge designs, then experiment with more colors!

Blending a bold color into white works really well, or how about blending two bright shades? Red and orange make a great sunset background.

tropical sunset

Try out the sponge technique with this totally tropical design. It's perfect for summer or vacation nails!

What you need:

- White nail polish
- Red nail polish
- Orange nail polish
- Yellow nail polish
- Black nail polish
- Two plastic straws
- Sponge

Before you start painting, you'll need to cut your two straws, as shown below.

 Area to keep   Waste area

1 Make two cuts about 1 inch down from the top, as shown. Cut the waste area away. This straw is used for the palm leaf shapes.

Straw 1

2 Make cuts in exactly the same way as you did with the other straw, but leave less of the straw remaining. This straw is used for the palm trunk.

Straw 2

Paint your nails using
white nail polish.

Take your sponge and paint three
stripes onto it using red, then orange,
then yellow nail polish.

Use the sponge technique to
transfer the design onto your nail.
Repeat step 2 and 3 for every nail.

Use straw 1 like a dotting tool
with black nail polish to add
a palm leaf. Press lightly
to create a half-moon shape.

Add two more half-moon
shapes to create half
of the palm leaves.

Add three more half-moon
shapes on the opposite side to
finish the top of the palm tree.

Use straw 2 to draw in the tree trunk
with black nail polish. Start between
the leaves and draw toward the tip.

Nail Designer

Use this space to practice before you paint and invent brand-new nail art. Doodle, color, and write notes to come up with your own designs!

White base coat   Colored shapes   Zigzags

I call this design Crazy Pop Art ....

I call this design ....

I call this design ....

I call this design ....

I call this design ....

I call this design ....

I call this design ....

I call this design ....

I call this design ....

I call this design ....

I call this design ....

I call this design ....

I call this design ....

I call this design ....

I call this design ....

I call this design ....

I call this design ....

I call this design ....

I call this design ....

I call this design ....

I call this design ....

I call this design ....

I call this design ....

I call this design ....

I call this design ....

I call this design ....

I call this design ....

I call this design ....

I call this design ....

I call this design ....

I call this design ....

I call this design ....

Say cheese!

Create a photo gallery of your favorite nail designs.
Stick in pictures of you and your friends to showcase your amazing nails!

My best friend with her
lovely leopard-print nails!

Fruity Fun

This super-sweet design is perfect for hot summer days. If you can't do the design on all your nails, why not just try one?

Go to page 22 to learn how to use nail stencils.

What you need:

- White nail polish
- Pink nail polish
- Green nail polish
- Black nail polish
- Stencil strips
- Dotting tool

Let's Get Started:

The watermelon design looks great in any tropical color!
Can you think of any other fruity designs?

Red

Pink

Green

Orange

1

Paint your nails using
white nail polish.

 2

Apply the stencil strip just
below the tip of your nails. It
should hang over both sides.

 3

Carefully paint pink nail polish on
the bottom section of your nails, making
sure you only go up to the strip.

 4

Paint green polish on the tips
of your nails. Again, make sure
you only go up to the strip.

 5

Carefully peel off the strip
in an upward direction.

 6

Use your dotting tool and black
nail polish to add a short line to the
middle of your nails, as shown.

 7

Add another short line to one side of the first.

Tip: Starting in the middle
will make your seeds even.

 8

Add the last short line
to the other side of the first
to complete the design.

Totally Tropical
Give these pineapples big personalities!

I'm a
cool dude!

Hoot-iful!

Twit-twoo! Create a little friend on each nail with this charming design.

What you need:

- Brown nail polish
- White nail polish
- Dark yellow nail polish
- Black nail polish
- Orange nail polish
- Dotting tool

Use a toothpick or a bobby pin if you don't have a dotting tool.

Let's Get Started:

1

Paint your nails using brown nail polish.

2

Paint a blob to cover about half of each nail using white nail polish, as shown.

Hint: The blob is the owl's tummy so it doesn't need to be perfect!

3

Use your dotting tool and dark yellow nail polish to add two large circles, as shown.

Tip: Go to page 10 for a reminder of how to use your dotting tool.

4

Clean your dotting tool and use it again with white nail polish to add dots in each dark yellow circle.

5

Use the smaller end of your dotting tool with black nail polish to add dots for eyes, and little lines to the tummy.

6

Clean your dotting tool and use it again with orange nail polish to add the beak and feet, as shown.

Unique Owls

You don't have to make your owls look like the real thing! Have fun creating owl creatures in weird and wonderful colors.

1 Follow the steps for the Hoot-iful! design but pick different color combinations.

2 Remember: lighter colors will stand out well against darker ones, but you may need two coats of the lighter color.

Perfect Penguins

These adorable penguins will give
any outfit the awwwww-factor!

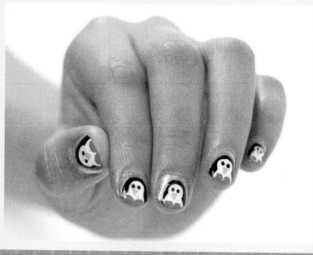

What you need:

- Glitter nail polish
- Black nail polish
- White nail polish
- Orange nail polish
- Yellow nail polish
- Dotting tool

Let's Get Started:

 1

Paint your nails
using glitter polish.

2

Paint a blob to cover most of each
nail using black nail polish, as shown.

Hint: You could use silver nail
polish if you don't have glitter.

3

Use white nail polish to paint the white part of the body, as shown.

Tip: Just paint a small white blob if you can't get the shape quite right.

 4

Use your dotting tool and orange nail polish to add the feet.

 5

Clean your dotting tool and use it again with black nail polish to add two dots for the eyes.

 6

Clean your dotting tool and use it again with yellow nail polish to add a beak.

Penguin Pals

Penguins look cute in different colors. How about experimenting to create quirky characters?

 1 This sweet penguin has a pastel pink body and feet.

2 This penguin is super-cozy in his woolen bobble hat.

3 This super-smart penguin is wearing a bow tie!

 59

Starry Sky

Fill the night sky with sparkling and shooting stars!

Starry Night

This magical midnight design is really fun to create and it looks super-special if you use pearly or glitter nail polish!

What you need:

- Pearly or glitter blue nail polish
- White nail polish
- Dotting tool
- A pencil with an eraser on the end

Add a few stars from your sticker sheet for a quick fix!

Create magical galaxy fingernails by changing the background colors. If you don't have pearly or glitter nail polish, try adding a glitter top coat instead of a clear one.

Green

Orange

Pink

Purple

Paint your nails using
the blue nail polish.

Paint your nails using
the blue nail polish.

Use your dotting tool and white
nail polish to draw a star, as shown.
The star is made up of four lines.

Use the eraser on the end of
your pencil like a dotting tool with white
nail polish to create the moon.

Use the dotting tool again
to add one or two tiny crosses.

Use your dotting tool to add
one or two tiny crosses.

Use the dotting tool again to add
tiny dots to the background.

Use the dotting tool again to add
tiny dots to the background.

Blob Creations

Turn these random spills into cute doodle characters!